The Best Jokes Book For Kids

Over 900 jokes, riddles, tongue twisters, knock knock jokes and limericks that children will love.

M. PREFONTAINE

D1439756

Contents

CHAPTER 1 JOKES

Q: Why did Jimmy's parents scream when they saw his report card?

A: There was a bee on it.

Q: What do you get if you throw all the books into the ocean?

A: A title wave

Q: Why do dragons sleep during the day?

A: So they can fight knights

Q: What did one wall say to the other wall?

A: I'll meet you at the corner

Q: What do you call the heavy breathing someone makes while trying to hold a yoga pose?

A: Yoga pants.

Q: What do you call a guy who never farts in public?

A: A private tutor

Q: What do you call a boomerang that never comes back?

A: *A stick*

Q: What did the tomato say to the mushroom?

A: *"You look like a fungi."*

Q: What does a rain cloud wear under its clothes?

A: *Thunderwear*

Q: What did the alien say to the flowerbed?

A: *Take me to your weeder.*

Q: What do bees do if they want to use public transport?

A: *Wait at a buzz stop*

Q: Why shouldn't you write with a broken pencil?

A: *Because it's pointless.*

Q: What lies at the bottom of the ocean and twitches?

A: *A nervous wreck*

Q: Why was the broom late for school?

A: *It over-swept.*

Q: What's the difference between broccoli and bogey's?

A: Kids won't eat broccoli.

Q: Why was the sewing machine so funny?

A: It kept everyone in stitches.

Q: How does a mouse feel after it takes a shower?

A: Squeaky clean.

Q: What do you call a cow in a tornado?

A: A milkshake.

Q: How do you catch a squirrel?

A: Climb up a tree and act like a nut

Q: What do you call a guy who lays in front of a door?

A: Matt

Q: What do you have if your dog can't bark?

A: Hush puppy.

Q: What's a snake's favorite school subject.

A: Hiss-tory

Q: Why did the horse keep falling over?

A: It just wasn't stable.

Q: Why was the elf crying?

A: He stubbed his mistle-toe.

Q: What do you call two rows of vegetables?

A: A dual cabbage way.

Q: Why did the banana go to the doctor?

A: Because it wasn't peeling well.

Q: What did the tooth fairy use to fix her wand?

A: Toothpaste.

Q: What do you call an angry pea?

A: Grump-pea.

Q: Why did the spider go on the internet?

A: To make a Webpage.

Q: What illness do martial artists get?

A: Kung - Flu.

Q: What did the baby corn say to the Mum corn?

A: Where's Popcorn

Q: Where do baby apes sleep?

A: In apricots

Q: What game do elephants love to play?

A: Squash

Q: Why do fish live in salt water?

A: Because pepper makes them sneeze

Q: What did the mother ghost say her children?

A: Don't spook until you're spooken to.

Q: Why do witches wear name tags?

A: So that they can tell witch is which.

Q: What do witches put on their hair?

A: Scare spray.

Q: When is it bad luck to meet a black cat?

A: When you're a mouse.

Q: What happened when a boy vampire met a girl vampire?

A: It was love at first bite

Q: What's a skeleton's favorite musical instrument?

A: A trom-bone

Q: Where do baby ghosts go during the day?

A: Dayscare centres.

Q: Why don't skeletons like parties?

A: They have no body to dance with.

Q: Who did Frankenstein take to the prom?

A: His ghoul friend.

Q: What kind of streets do zombies like to haunt?

A: Dead end streets.

Q: What has webbed feet, feathers, fangs and goes quack-quack?

A: Count duckula.

Q: How do astronauts serve dinner?

A: On flying saucers.

Q: What's worse than raining cats and dogs?

A: Hailing taxi's

Q: How do you make an artichoke?

A: Strangle it

Q: What's a scarecrow's favorite fruit?

A: Strawberries.

Q: Why can't the elephant use the computer?

A: Because he's afraid of the mouse.

Q: What do ghosts use to wash their hair?

A: Sham-BOO.

Q: Why did Dracula's mother give him cough medicine?

A: Because he was having a coffin fit.

Q: What did Dr. Frankenstein get when he put a goldfish brain in the body of his dog?

A: Don't know, but it is great at chasing submarines.

Q: Why wasn't there any food left after the monster party?'

A: Because everyone was a goblin.

Q: What did the triangle say to the circle?

A: I don't see your point.

Q: What is a vampires favorite holiday?

A: Fangsgiving.

Q: What do skeletons say before they begin dining?

A: Bone appetite

Q: What is a ghoul's favourite drink?

A: Slime juice

Q: What do fishermen say on Halloween?

A: 'Trick-or-trout'

Q: Where do spooks go to post a parcel?

A: The ghost office.

Q: What did the vampire say to the Invisible Man?

A: Long time, no see

Q: What did the squirrel give for Valentine's Day?

A: Forget-me-nuts.

Q: What do you call two birds in love?

A: Tweet-hearts.

Q: What did the calculator say to the other calculator on Valentine's Day?

A: Let me count the ways I love you.

Q: What did one piece of string say to the other piece of string?

A: Will you be my Valen-twine?

Q: Why can't skeletons play music?

A: Because they have no organs.

Q: What do you call an elephant in a phone booth?

A: Stuck

Q: What did the spoon say to the knife?

A: You're so sharp

Q: How did the hairdresser win the race?

A: She knew a shortcut.

Q: What do witches order at hotels?

A: Broom service.

Q: Why did the Cyclops stop teaching?

A: *Because he only had one pupil.*

Q: Why didn't Dracula have any friends?

A: *Because he was a pain in the neck.*

Q: Where did the witch have to go when she misbehaved?

A: *To her broom.*

Q: What's a ghost's favorite room in the house?

A: *The living room.*

Q: What do birds do on Halloween?

A: *They go trick or tweeting.*

Q: Which monster is the best dance partner?

A: *The Boogie Man.*

Q: Which side of the turkey has the most feathers?

A: *The outside.*

Q: What type of diet did the snowman go on?

A: *The Meltdown Diet.*

Q: What did the snowman have for breakfast?

A: *Frosted Flakes.*

Q: What happened to the man who stole a calendar from the store?

A: *He got 12 months.*

Q: Why was Santa's helper sad?

A: *Because he had low elf-esteem.*

Q: What does Santa clean his sleigh with?

A: *Comet.*

Q: What did the paper clip say to the magnet?

A: *I find you very attractive.*

Q: What's a ghost's favorite fruit?

A: *Boo-berries.*

Q: Why did the robber take a shower?

A: *Because he wanted to make a clean getaway.*

Q: What do you call a shoe made from a banana?

A: *A slipper.*

Q: Why are there fences around cemeteries?

A: Because people are dying to get in.

Q: What do you call a fish with no eye?

A: A fsh.

Q: What do gymnasts, acrobats, and bananas all have in common?

A: They can all do splits.

Q: What day of the week does the potato look forward to the least?

A: Fry-day.

Q: What is Dracula's favorite fruit?

A: Neck-tarines.

Q: What does a skeleton order for dinner?

A: Spare ribs.

Q: Where does the witch park her vehicle?

A: In the broom closet.

Q: Why couldn't the ghost see his parents?

A: Because they were trans-parents.

Q: What did the cow say on December 25th?

A: *Mooey Christmas*

Q: Why didn't the turkey have any Christmas dinner?

A: *Because he was stuffed.*

Q: What did the snowman say to the other snowman?

A: *Can you smell carrots?*

Q: What sneaks around the kitchen on Christmas Eve?

A: *Mince spies.*

Q: How do you make a tissue dance?

A: *You put a little boogie in it.*

Q: Why can't you hear a pterodactyl in the bathroom?

A: *Because it has a silent pee.*

Q: What does a nosey pepper do?

A: *Gets jalapeno business*

Q: What do you call a deer with no eyes?

A: No eye deer.

Q: What do you call a deer with no eyes and no legs?

A: Still no eye deer.

Q: The past, present and future walk into a bar.

A: It was tense.

Q: Why was Tigger looking in the toilet?

A: He was looking for Pooh.

Q: What do you get when you throw a piano down a mine shaft?

A: A flat miner.

Q: What do you get when you put a candle in a suit of armor?

A: A knight light.

Q: What did the 0 say to the 8?

A: Nice belt

Q: Why did the orange stop?

A: Because, it ran outta juice.

Q: Why did the stop light turn red?

A: You would too if you had to change in the middle if the street

Q: What did the green grape say to the purple grape?

A: Breathe

Q: If you're American in the living room, what are you in the bathroom?

A: European

Q: What kind of cats like to go bowling?

A: Alley cats.

Q: What kind of eggs does a wicked chicken lay?

A: Deviled eggs.

Q: What lies on its back, with one hundred feet in the air?

A: A dead centipede.

Q: What's gray, eats fish, and lives in Washington, D.C.?

A: The Presidential Seal.

Q: What's green and loud?

A: A froghorn

Q: What's round and bad-tempered?

A: A vicious circle

Q: What's the best thing to put into a pie?

A: Your teeth.

Q: What did the nut say when it got a cold?

A: Cashew

Q: What is it called when a cat wins a dog show?

A: A cat-has-trophy

Q: What do you call a sleeping bull?

A: A bulldozer.

Q: What do you call a sheep with no head or legs?

A: A cloud.

Q: What season is it when you go on a trampoline?

A: Springtime.

Q: Why does Waldo were stripes?

A: Because he doesn't want to be spotted.

Q: What kind of dog can do magic tricks?

A: It was a labracadabrador.

Q: Did you hear about the thieves that broke into the police station last night and stole all the toilets.

A: A police spokesman said the police have nothing to go on.

Q: What happened when Elma tried to catch some fog.

A: I mist.

Q: What's red and bad for your teeth?

A: A brick.

Q: What did the volcano say to his wife?

A: I lava you so much.

Q. Why did the alien want to leave the party?

A: The atmosphere wasn't right.

Q. What is an astronauts favorite snack?

A: Space Chips.

Q. What's an aliens favorite candy?

A: Martian-mellows.

Q. What's an astronauts favorite drink?

A: Gravi-tea.

Q. What did one eye say to the other?

A: Between me and you, something smells.

Q. Why don't acrobats work in the winter?

A: They only do Summer-saults.

Q. What monkey is always exploding?

A: A ba-boom.

Q: What is black and white and spins around?

A: A zebra stuck in a revolving door.

Q: What did one toilet say to the other?

A: You look a bit flushed.

Q: Why do bicycles fall over?

A: Because they are two-tired

Q: What did the stamp say to the envelope?

A: Stick with me and we will go places

Q: Why couldn't the pirate play cards?

A: Because he was sitting on the deck

Q: How do all the oceans say hello to each other?

A: They wave

Q: What is the difference between elephants and grapes?

A: Grapes are purple.

Q: Why did the picture go to jail?

A: Because it was framed.

Q: Were you long in the hospital?

A: No, I was the same size I am now

Q: Why was the belt arrested?

A: Because it held up some pants!

Q: How do you know if there's an elephant under your bed?

A: Your head hits the ceiling

Q: Why are elephants so wrinkled?

A: Because they take too long to iron

Q: How do you keep an elephant from charging?

A: Take away her credit card

Q: Why did the elephant paint himself different colors?

A: So he could hide in the crayon box

Q: What do you call a cow with no legs?

A: Ground beef

Q: What do you call a pig that knows karate?

A: A pork chop

Q: What animal needs to wear a wig?

A: A bald eagle

Q: What do you call an alligator in a vest?

A: An investigator

Q: Why did the math book look so sad?

A: Because it had so many problems

Q: Can a kangaroo jump higher than the Empire State Building?

A: Of course! The Empire State Building can't jump

Q: Why do bees have sticky hair?

A: Because they use honeycombs

Q: Why is 6 afraid of 7?

A: Because 7 8 9

Q: What's black and white, black and white, black and white?

A: A penguin rolling down a hill

Q: How did the barber win the race?

A: He knew a short cut.

Q: Did you hear about the pregnant bed-bug?

A: She's having her babies in the spring.

Q: Which is the best athlete to have with you on a cold day?

A: A long jumper.

Q: Did you hear about the two men arrested for stealing batteries and fireworks?

A: One was charged but the other was let off.

Q: What does an octopus wear in the winter?

A: A coat of arms.

Q: What bird is always out of breath?

A: A puffin.

Q: What do you get when you cross a Bear and Skunk?

A: Winnie the Pehew

Q: What's the biggest moth in the world?

A: Mam-moth.

Q: What is a mosquito's favorite sport?

A: Skin-diving.

Q: Why couldn't the chicken find her eggs?

A: She mislaid them

Q: What jam can't be eaten on toast?

A: A traffic jam

Q: What kind of food is crazy about money?

A: A dough-nut

Q: Which bean do kids like best?

A: The Jellybean.

Q: Why did the man go into the pizza business?

A: He wanted to make some dough.

Q: What do porcupines say after they kiss?

A: Ouch

Q: What does a cat like to eat on a hot summer's day?

A: A mice cream cone.

Q: Which are the strongest creatures in the ocean?

A: Mussels.

Q: What do you call Rodents that play Hockey?

A: Rink Rats

Q: Why did the lion spit out the clown?

A: Because he tasted funny.

Q: What is the best way to communicate with a fish?

A: Drop it a line

Q: What did the water say to the boat?

A: Nothing, it just waved.

Q: What did the fish say when he swam into the wall?

A: Dam

Q: Why don't skeletons fight each other?

A: They don't have the guts.

Q: How do dinosaurs pay their bills?

A: With Tyrannosaurus checks.

Q: What do you call a dinosaur that smashes everything in its path?

A: Tyrannosaurus wrecks.

Q: How do you make an egg laugh?

A: Tell it a yolk.

Q: What bird can lift the most?

A: A crane.

Q: What bone will a dog never eat?

A: A trombone.

Q: What clothes does a house wear?

A: Address.

Q: What country makes you shiver?

A: Chile.

Q: What did one elevator say to the other?

A: I think I'm coming down with something

Q: What did one magnet say to the other?

A: I find you very attractive.

Q: What did the necktie say to the hat?

A: You go on ahead. I'll hang around for a while.

Q: What did the rug say to the floor?

A: Don't move, I've got you covered.

Q: What do bees do with their honey?

A: They cell it.

Q: Why were the teacher's eyes crossed?

A: She couldn't control her pupils.

Q: What do you get if you cross an insect with the Easter rabbit?

A: Bugs Bunny.

Q: What happened when the spider got a new car?

A: He took it for a spin.

Q: What type of music does a boulder like?

A: Rock-n-roll.

Q: Why did the ice cream cone want to be a reporter?

A: He wanted to get the scoop.

Q: How do you get a tissue to dance?

A: Put a little boogie in it.

Q: Why was the metal wire so upset?

A: He was getting bent out of shape over nothing.

Q: How did the orange get into a crowded restaurant?

A: He squeezed his way in.

Q: Why can't a bank keep a secret?

A: It has too many tellers.

Q: What do you call the story about three little pigs?

A: A pigtail.

Q: Why did the hamburger lose the race?

A: It couldn't ketchup.

Q: What do you call a fairy who won't take a bath?

A: Stinkerbell.

Q: Why did the cookie complain about being ill?

A: He was feeling crummy.

Q: What's the craziest bird in the world?

A: A coo-coo.

Q: What kind of bees never die?

A: Zom-bees.

Q: What do you call a lazy kangaroo?

A: A pouch potato

Q: Why are frogs always so happy?

A: They eat everything that bugs them.

Q: Why did the pony get sent to her room without supper?

A: Because she kept horsing around.

Q: Why was the deer, the rabbit and the weasel laughing so much?

A: Because the owl was a hoot.

Q: What do you call an insect that complains all the time?

A: A grumble-bee.

Q: What's a sheep's favorite meal?

A: A bah-bah-que

Q: How do sea creatures communicate under water?

A: With shell phones.

Q: Who makes fish wishes come true?

A: Fairy cod-mother.

Q: What's the Worlds Hungriest animal?

A: A turkey is as it just gobble, gobble, gobbles.

Q: When do you have to ask hamburgers lots of questions?

A: When you want to grill them.

Q: What's a duck's favorite snack?

A: Cheese and quackers.

Q: What do you call a cow afraid of everything?

A: A cow-ard.

Q: What do you call a bear with no teeth?

A: A gummy bear!

Q: What do you call cheese that isn't yours?

A: Nacho cheese

Q: Where do cows go for entertainment?

A: To the moo-vies

Q: What does a snail say when it's riding on a turtle's back?

A: Weeeee

Q: Why did the jelly baby go to school?

A: Because he really wanted to be a smartie.

Q: What bug is welcome in apartments?

A: Ten-ants.

Q: Where do ants eat?

A: At a restaur-ant.

Q: What is the biggest ant in the world?

A: An eleph-ant.

Q: Who led ten thousand pigs up the hill and back down again?

A: The grand old duke of pork.

Q: Who shouted 'Knickers' at the big bad wolf?

A: Little rude riding hood.

Q: How did the sheep feel when little bo peep lost them?

A: Baaaaaad really Baaaaaad.

Q: What's the hardest thing about learning to ride a bike?

A: The ground.

Q: Why couldn't the biscuit find its way home?

A: It had been wafer too long.

Q: How do you know which end of a worm is its head?

A: Tickle its tummy and see which end laughs.

Q: What do you call a duck with a huge ice cream?

A: A lucky ducky

Q: what do you call the duck after he dropped in on his head?

A: A mucky ducky

Q: What's covered in custard and always complains?

A: Apple grumble

Q: Why did the swordfish blush?

A: Because the sea weed.

Q: What do you get if you blow hot air down a rabbit hole?

A: Hot cross bunnies.

Q: Why did the can crusher quit his job?

A: Because it was soda pressing.

Q: How do snails fight?

A: They slug it out.

Q: Why do bananas wear suntan lotion?

A: Because they peel.

Q: Why are penguins socially awkward?

A: Because they can't break the ice.

Q: Where do hamburgers go to dance?

A: They go to the meat-ball

Q: What kind of shoes do all spies wear?

A: Sneakers

Q: What did the penny say to the other penny?

A: We make perfect cents.

Q: How do you find a Princess?

A: You follow the foot Prince.

Q: Why do abcdefghijklmopqrstuvwxy & z hate hanging out with the letter n?

A: Because n always has to be the center of attention.

Q: What do you call someone who is afraid of Santa?

A: A Clausterphobic

Q. What's invisible and smells of Carrots?

A: Rabbit farts

Q: Where do cows hang their paintings?

A: In the mooo-seum.

Q: Why does a Moon-rock taste better than an Earth-rock?

A: Because it's a little meteor

Q: What did the buffalo say to his son when he left for college?

A: Bison

Chapter 2 Knock Knock Jokes

Knock, knock.
Who's there?
Canoe.
Canoe who?
Canoe come out and play with me today?

Knock, knock.
Who's there?
Honey bee.
Honey bee who?
Honey bee a dear and get me some juice.

Knock, knock.
Who's there?
Cow says.
Cow says who?
No silly, a cow says Mooooo

Knock, knock.
Who's there?
Mikey.
Mikey who?
Mikey doesn't fit in the keyhole.

Knock, knock.
Who's there?
Interrupting cow.
Interrup...Moooooooooo!

Knock, knock.
Who's there?
Lettuce.
Lettuce who?
Lettuce in, it's cold out here.

Knock, knock.
Who's there?
Wooden shoe.
Wooden shoe who?
Wooden shoe like to hear another joke?

Knock, knock.
Who's there?
Watson.
Watson who?
What's on TV tonight?

Knock, knock.
Who's there?
Atch.
Atch who?
Bless you.

Knock, knock.
Who's there?
A broken pencil.
A broken pencil who?
Oh never mind it's pointless.

Knock, Knock.
Who's there?

Who.
Who who?
Are you an owl?

Knock, Knock.
Who's there?
Cash.
Cash who?
I knew you were a nut.

Knock, knock.
Who's there?
Tank.
Tank who?
Your welcome.

Knock, knock!
Who's there?
Annie.
Annie who?
Annie body home?

Knock, knock.
Who's there?
Cook.
Cook who?
Hey! Who are you calling cuckoo?

Knock, knock.
Who's there?
Spell.
Spell who?
W-H-O.

Knock, knock
Who's there?
Iva.
Iva who?
I've a sore hand from knocking.

Knock, knock.
Who's there?
Avenue.
Avenue who?
Avenue knocked on this door before?

Knock, knock.
Who's there?
Ice cream.
Ice cream who?
Ice cream if you don't let me in.

Knock, knock.
Who's there?
A titch.
A titch who?
Bless you.

Knock, knock.
Who's there?
Goat.
Goat who?
Goat to the door and find out.

Knock, knock.
Who's there?

Howard.
Howard who?
Howard I know?

Knock, knock.
Who's there?
Nobel.
Nobel who?
No bell, that's why I knocked.

Knock, knock.
Who's there?
Me.
Me who?
Wow! You don't know who you are?

Knock, knock.
Who's there?
Hawaii.
Hawaii who?
I'm fine. Hawaii you.

Knock, knock.
Who's There?
Theodore.
Theodore who?
Theodore is stuck and it won't open.

Knock, Knock.
Who's there?
Russell.
Russell who?
Russell up something to eat.

Knock, Knock.
Who's there?
Doughnut.
Doughnut Who?
Doughnut ask, it's a secret.

Knock, Knock.
Who's there?
Ya.
Ya Who?
What are you so excited about?

Knock, Knock.
Who's there?
I am.
I am who?
You don't know who you are?

Knock, Knock.
Who's there.
Tuna.
Tuna who?
You can tuna piano, but you can't tuna fish.

Knock, Knock.
Who's there?
Vlad.
Vlad who?
Vlad to meet you.

Knock, Knock
Who's there.
Greece.

Greece who.
Greece my palm and I'll tell you.

Knock, Knock.
Who's there?
Voodoo.
Voodoo who?
Voodoo you think you are?

Knock, Knock.
Who's there?
Heaven.
Heaven who?
Heaven seen you for a long time.

Knock, Knock.
Who's there?
Kenya.
Kenya who?
Kenya guess who is it?

Knock, Knock.
Who's there?
Russian.
Russian who?
Russian about makes me tired.

Knock, Knock.
Who's there?
Miles.
Miles who?
Miles away.

Knock, Knock.
Who's there?
Modem.
Modem who?
Modem lawns, grass is getting high.

Knock, Knock.
Who's there?
Nana.
Nana who?
Nana your business.

Knock, Knock.
Who's there?
Philip.
Philip who?
Philip my glass will you please.

Knock, Knock.
Who's there?
Pudding.
Pudding who?
Pudding on your shoes before your trousers is a
bad idea.

Knock, Knock.
Who's there?
Rain.
Rain who?
Rain dear, you know, Rudolph the red nosed rain
dear.

Knock, Knock.
Who's there?
Safari.
Safari who?
Safari so good.

Knock, Knock.
Who's there?
Sharon.
Sharon who?
Sharon share alike.

Knock, Knock.
Who's there?
Sid.
Sid who?
Sid down and have a cup of tea.

Knock, Knock.
Who's there?
Sinker.
Sinker who?
Sinker swim, it's up to you.

Knock, Knock.
Who's there?
Thermos.
Thermos who?
Thermos be a better knock knock joke than this.

Knock, Knock.
Who's there?

Thistle.
Thistle who?
Thistle be the last time I knock on this door.

Knock, Knock.
Who's there?
Carrie.
Carrie who?
Carrie me home, I'm tired.

Knock, Knock
Who's there?
Cliff.
Cliff who?
Cliff hanger.

Knock, Knock
Who's there?
Stan.
Stan who?
Stan back, I'm knocking the door down.

Knock, Knock.
Who's there?
Tuba.
Tuba who?
Tuba toothpaste.

Knock, Knock.
Who's there?
Witches.
Witches who?
Witches the way to go home.

Knock, Knock.
Who's there?
Yee.
Yee who?
What? Are you a cowboy?

Knock, Knock.
Who's there?
Yukon.
Yukon who?
Yukon lead a horse to water, but you can't make it drink.

Knock, Knock.
Who's there?
Zoom.
Zoom who?
Zoom did you expect.

Knock, knock.
Who's there?
Water.
Water who?
Water way to answer the door.

Knock, Knock.
Who's there?
Broccoli.
Broccoli who?
Broccoli doesn't have a last name, silly.

Knock, Knock.
Who's there?
Justin.
Justin who?
Justin time for lunch.

Knock, knock.
Who's there?
Alex.
Alex who?
Alex-plain later.

Knock, knock.
Who's there?
CD.
CD who?
CD guy on your doorstep?

Knock, Knock.
Who's there?
Denise.
Denise who?
Denise are above your ankles.

Knock, Knock.
Who's there?
Sacha.
Sacha who?
Sacha lot of questions.

Knock, Knock.
Who's there?

Des.
Des who?
Des no bell, dat's why I'm knocking.

Knock, Knock.
Who's there?
Diesel.
Diesel who?
Diesel make you feel better.

Knock, Knock.
Who's there?
Sam.
Sam who?
Sam person who knocked on the door last time.

Knock, Knock.
Who's there?
Dishes.
Dishes who?
Dishes a very bad joke.

Knock, Knock.
Who's there?
Dismay.
Dismay who?
Dismay be a joke but it doesn't make me laugh.

Knock, knock.
Who's there?
Scot.
Scot who?
Scot nothing to do with you.

46

Knock, Knock.
Who's there?
Doctor.
Doctor who?
That's right - where's my tardis?

Knock, Knock.
Who's there?
Sandy.
Sandy who?
Sandy door, I just got a splinter.

Knock, Knock.
Who's there?
Duck.
Duck who?
Just duck. They're throwing things at us.

Knock, knock.
Who's there?
Isabel.
Isabel who?
Isabel working? I had to knock.

Knock, Knock.
Who's there?
Alec.
Alec who?
Alec-tricity. Isn't that a shock?

Knock, Knock.
Who's there?

Duke.
Duke who?
Duke come here often.

Knock, Knock.
Who's there?
Alec.
Alec who?
Alec my lolly.

Knock, Knock.
Who's there?
Alison.
Alison who?
Alison Wonderland.

Knock, Knock.
Who's there?
Dwight.
Dwight who?
Dwight way and the wrong way.

Knock, Knock.
Who's there?
Alma.
Alma who?
Alma not going to tell you.

Knock, Knock.
Who's there?
Dan.
Dan who?
Dan Druff.

48

Knock, Knock.
Who's there?
Alpaca.
Alpaca who?
Alpaca picnic lunch.

Knock, Knock.
Who's there?
Dana.
Dana who?
Dana talk with your mouth full.

Knock, Knock.
Who's there?
Amahl.
Amahl who?
Amahl shook up.

Knock, Knock.
Who's there?
Datsun.
Datsun who?
Datsun old joke.

Knock, Knock.
Who's there?
Ammonia.
Ammonia who?
Ammonia little boy who can't reach the doorbell.

Knock, Knock.
Who's there?

Della.
Della who?
Della-katessen.

Knock, Knock.
Who's there?
Annie.
Annie who?
Annie-versary.

Knock, Knock.
Who's there?
Attila.
Attila who?
Attila you no lies.

Knock, Knock.
Who's there?
Auntie.
Auntie who?
Auntie glad to see me again.

Knock, Knock.
Who's there?
Ear.
Ear who?
Ear you are, I've been looking for you.

Knock, Knock.
Who's there?
Bee.
Bee who?
Bee careful.

Knock, Knock.
Who's there?
Frank.
Frank who?
Frankenstien.

Knock, Knock.
Who's there?
Ears.
Ears who?
Ears looking at you.

Knock, Knock.
Who's there?
Bacon.
Bacon who?
Bacon a cake for your birthday.

Knock, Knock.
Who's there?
Ellie.
Ellie who?
Ellie Phants never forget.

Knock, Knock.
Who's there?
Boo.
Boo who?
Just Boo. I'm a ghost.

Knock, Knock.
Who's there?

Bet.
Bet who?
Bet you don't know who's knocking on your door.

Knock, Knock
Who's there?
Barbie.
Barbie who?
Barbie Q.

Knock, Knock.
Who's there?
Flea.
Flea who?
Flea's a jolly good fellow.

Knock, Knock.
Who's there?
Furry.
Furry who?
Furry's a jolly good fellow.

Knock, Knock.
Who's there?
Ho-ho.
Ho-ho who?
You know, your Santa impression could use a
little work.

Knock, Knock
Who's there?

Chile.
Chile who?
Chile out tonight.

Knock, Knock.
Who's there?
Snow.
Snow who?
Snow use. I forgot my name again.

Knock, Knock
Who's there?
Colleen.
Colleen who?
Colleen up your room, it's filthy.

Knock, Knock.
Who's there?
Gus.
Gus who?
That's what you're supposed to do.

Knock, Knock.
Who's there?
Hal.
Hal who?
Hallo to you too.

Knock, knock.
Who's there?
Cows go.
Cows go who?
No you idiot, cows go mooo.

Knock, knock.
Who's there?
Kanga.
Kanga who?
Actually, it's kangaroo.

Knock, knock.
Who's there?
Beats.
Beats who?
Beats me.

Knock, knock.
Who's there?
Dozen.
Dozen who?
Dozen all this knocking bother you already?

Knock, Knock
Who's there?
Augusta.
Augusta who?
Augusta wind will blow the witch away.

Chapter 3 Tongue Twisters

Peter Piper picked a peck of pickled peppers. A peck of pickled peppers Peter Piper picked. If Peter Piper picked a peck of pickled peppers, Where's the peck of pickled peppers Peter Piper picked?

How can a clam cram in a clean cream can?

Sheena leads, Sheila needs.
Sheena leads, Sheila needs.
Sheena leads, Sheila needs.

Seth at Sainsbury's sells thick socks.

Clean clams crammed in clean cans.

Six sick hicks nick six slick bricks with picks and sticks.

Luke Luck likes lakes. Luke's duck likes lakes. Luke Luck licks lakes. Luck's duck licks lakes. Duck takes licks in lakes Luke Luck likes. Luke Luck takes licks in lakes duck likes.

Seventy-seven benevolent elephants

Willy's real rear wheel

Did Dick Pickens prick his pinkie pickling cheap cling peaches in an inch of Pinch or framing his famed French finch photos?

When you write copy you have the right to copyright the copy you write

Hassock hassock, black spotted hassock. Black spot on a black back of a black spotted hassock.

How many cookies could a good cook cook If a good cook could cook cookies? A good cook could cook as much cookies as a good cook who could cook cookies.

Mary Mac's mother's making Mary Mac marry me. My mother's making me marry Mary Mac. Will I always be so Merry when Mary's taking care of me? Will I always be so merry when I marry Mary Mac?

She saw Sheriff's shoes on the sofa. But was she so sure she saw Sherif's shoes on the sofa?

Through three cheese trees three free fleas flew. While these fleas flew, freezy breeze blew. Freezy breeze made these three trees freeze. Freezy trees made these trees' cheese freeze. That's what made these three free fleas sneeze.

Black background, brown background.
Black background, brown background.
Black background, brown background.

Tie twine to three tree twigs.
Tie twine to three tree twigs.
Tie twine to three tree twigs.

Rory the warrior and Roger the worrier were
reared wrongly in a rural brewery

Three short sword sheaths.
Three short sword sheaths.
Three short sword sheaths.

Green glass globes glow greenly.

As I was in Arkansas I saw a saw that could out
saw any saw I ever saw saw. If you happen to be in
Arkansas and see a saw that can out saw the saw I
saw saw I'd like to see the saw you saw saw.

Red Buick, blue Buick
Red Buick, blue Buick
Red Buick, blue Buick

Rhys watched Ross switch his Irish wristwatch for
a Swiss wristwatch.

Near an ear, a nearer ear, a nearly eerie ear.

On a lazy laser raiser lies a laser ray eraser.

Scissors sizzle, thistles sizzle.

How much caramel can a canny canonball cram in a camel if a canny canonball can cram caramel in a camel?

He threw three free throws.

She sells seashells on the seashore.

Mix a box of mixed biscuits with a boxed biscuit mixer.

A proper copper coffee pot.

Six thick thistle sticks.
Six thick thistle sticks.
Six thick thistles stick.

The instinct of an extinct insect stinks.
The instinct of an extinct insect stinks.
The instinct of an extinct insect stinks.

Which wristwatches are Swiss wristwatches?

One-One was a racehorse.
Two-Two was one, too.
When One-One won one race,
Two-Two won one, too.

A good cook could cook as much cookies as a good cook who could cook cookies.

I saw a saw that could out saw any other saw I ever saw.

Betty Botter bought some butter, but she said "this butter's bitter But a bitof better butter will but make my butter better" So she bought some betterbutter, better than the bitter butter, and it made her butter better so 'twas

Black bug bit a big black bear. But where is the big black bear that the big black bug bit?

A big bug bit the little beetle but the little beetle bit the big bug back.

I wish to wish the wish you wish to wish, but if you wish the wish the witch wishes, I won't wish the wish you wish to wish.

These thousand tricky tongue twisters trip thrillingly off the tongue.

Betty bought butter but the butter was bitter, so Betty bought better butter to make the bitter butter better.

A sailor went to sea to see, what he could see. And all he could see was sea, sea, sea.

A box of mixed biscuits, a mixed biscuit box.

Purple Paper People, Purple Paper People, Purple Paper People

If two witches were watching two watches, which witch would watch which watch? ...sent by Richard Walsh.

Which watch did which witch wear and which witch wore which watch?

Six slippery snails, slid slowly seaward.

I thought a thought. But the thought I thought wasn't the thought I thought I thought. If the thought I thought I thought had been the thought I thought, I wouldn't have thought so much.

How much wood could a wood chuck; chuck if a wood chuck could chuck wood.

I scream, you scream, we all scream for ice cream

Any noise annoys an oyster but a noisy noise annoys an oyster more.

A skunk sat on a stump. The stump thought the skunk stunk. the skunk thought the stump stunk.

The owner of the inside inn was inside his inside inn with his inside outside his inside inn.

Baboon bamboo, baboon bamboo, baboon bamboo, baboon bamboo, baboon bamboo, baboon bamboo.

The thirty-three thieves thought that they thrilled the throne throughout Thursday.

Daddy draws doors.Daddy draws doors.Daddy draws doors.

Friendly Fleas and Fire Flies

Fuzzy Wuzzy was a bear, Fuzzy Wuzzy had no hair, FuzzyWuzzy wasn't very fuzzy.

How many cans can a canner can, if a canner can can cans? A canner can can as many cans as a canner can, if a canner can can cans.

If a black bug bleeds black blood, what color blood does a blue bug bleed?

If Freaky Fred Found Fifty Feet of Fruit and Fed Forty Feet to his Friend Frank how many Feet of Fruit did Freaky Fred Find?

Penny's pretty pink piggy bank
Penny's pretty pink piggy bank
Penny's pretty pink piggy bank

A tutor who tooted the flute, tried to tutor two tooters to toot. Said the two to the tutor, 'Is it harder to toot or to tutor two tooters to toot?'

One smart fellow, he felt smart. Two smart fellows, they felt smart. Three smart fellows, they all felt smart.

Crisp crusts crackle and crunch.
Crisp crusts crackle and crunch.
Crisp crusts crackle and crunch.

Tie a knot, tie a knot.
Tie a tight, tight knot.
Tie a knot in the shape of a naught.

Freshly-fried fat flying fish

Jolly juggling jesters jauntily juggled jingling jacks.

Kindly kittens knitting mittens keep kazooing in the king's kitchen.

Billy Button bought a buttered biscuit, did Billy Button buy a buttered biscuit? If Billy Button bought a buttered biscuit, Where's the buttered biscuit Billy Button bought?

She saw a fish on the seashore and I'm sure The fish she saw on the seashore was a saw-fish.

Swan swam over the sea,
Swim, swan, swim.
Swan swam back again
Well swum, swan.

If you tell Tom to tell a tongue-twister his tongue
will be twisted as tongue-twister twists tongues.

Mr. See owned a saw.
And Mr. Soar owned a seesaw.
Now See's saw sawed Soar's seesaw
Before Soar saw See,
Which made Soar sore.
Had Soar seen See's saw
Before See sawed Soar's seesaw,
See's saw would not have sawed
Soar's seesaw.
So See's saw sawed Soar's seesaw.
But it was sad to see Soar so sore
Just because See's saw sawed
Soar's seesaw.

I cannot bear to see a bear
Bear down upon a hare.
When bare of hair he strips the hare,
Right there I cry, "Forbear."

Silly Sally swiftly shooed seven silly sheep.
The seven silly sheep Silly Sally shooed
shilly-shallied south.

These sheep shouldn't sleep in a shack;
sheep should sleep in a shed.
You've no need to light a night-light.

On a light night like tonight,
For a night-light's light's a slight light,
And tonight's a night that's light.
When a night's light, like tonight's light,
It is really not quite right
To light night-lights with their slight lights
On a light night like tonight.

Of all the felt I ever felt,
I never felt a piece of felt
which felt as fine as that felt felt,
when first I felt that felt hat's felt.

The crowd of clumsy clowns crushed the king's
crown.

The detective discovered the deadly dagger in
Dad's dirty diapers.

The tiny teacher on tippytoes tamed the terrible
T-Rex by tickling its tummy.

Noisy boys enjoy noisy toys, but noisy boys
enjoying noisy toys are annoying.

The fat farmer's five filthy fingers fed the
ferocious ferret french fries.

Greedy Grandpa grabbed Grandma's greasy grubs.

The peppy puppy the prince presented the princess produced piles of poop in the palace.

The hippos heard the hunter's hiccups and hurried home to hide.

The big, bumbling bear burned his butt baking bread.

The twins took the toilet and tiptoed toward town to try trading it for toys.

My sister's shop sells shoes for sheep.
My sister's shop sells shoes for sheep.
My sister's shop sells shoes for sheep.

Firefighters found Father frowning from a funny fever and farting fierce flames.

The nervous nurse had another nasty nosebleed and needed nine napkins for her nostrils.

"Juicy!" joked the janitor, his jaws on the jiggling jellyfish.

If eight great apes ate eighty-eight grapes, guess how many grapes each great ape ate.

The little lambs, licking lollipops, went leaping and laughing into the lava.

When the wizard winked and waved his wand, the wars of the world went away.

Lesser leather never weathered wetter weather better.

What time does the wristwatch strap shop shut?

Old oily Ollie oils old oily autos.

I saw Susie sitting in a shoe shine shop. Where she sits she shines, and where she shines she sits.

How many boards
Could the Mongols hoard
If the Mongol hordes got bored?

Send toast to ten tense stout saints' ten tall tents.

Denise sees the fleece,
Denise sees the fleas.
At least Denise could sneeze
and feed and freeze the fleas

Something in a thirty-acre thermal thicket of thorns and thistles thumped and thundered threatening the three-D thoughts of Matthew the thug - although, theatrically, it was only the thirteen-thousand thistles and thorns through the underneath of his thigh that the thirty year old thug thought of that morning.

Six sick hicks nick six slick bricks with picks and sticks.

There was a fisherman named Fisher
who fished for some fish in a fissure.
Till a fish with a grin,
pulled the fisherman in.
Now they're fishing the fissure for Fisher.

Picky people pick Peter Pan Peanut-Butter, 'tis the peanut-butter picky people pick.

If Stu chews shoes, should Stu choose the shoes he chews?

Yellow butter, purple jelly, red jam, black bread.
Spread it thick, say it quick!
Yellow butter, purple jelly, red jam, black bread.
Spread it thicker, say it quicker!
Yellow butter, purple jelly, red jam, black bread.

Chester Cheetah chews a chunk of cheap cheddar cheese.

Real rock wall, real rock wall, real rock wall

Tommy Tucker tried to tie Tammy's Turtles tie.

A gazillion gigantic grapes gushed gradually giving gophers gooey guts.

If colored caterpillars could change their colours constantly could they keep their colored coat colored properly?

How much ground could a groundhog grind if a groundhog could grind ground?

How much myrtle would a wood turtle hurdle if a wood turtle could hurdle myrtle?

A wood turtle would hurdle as much myrtle as a wood turtle could hurdle if a wood turtle could hurdle myrtle.

How much dew does a dewdrop drop
If dewdrops do drop dew?
They do drop, they do
As do dewdrops drop
If dewdrops do drop dew.

Bake big batches of bitter brown bread.

While we were walking, we were watching window washers wash Washington's windows with warm washing water.

How much oil boil can a gum boil boil if a gum boil can boil oil?

No nose knows like a gnome's nose knows.

There are two minutes difference from four to
two to two to two, from two to two to two, too.

Ripe white wheat reapers reap ripe white wheat
right.

Blake's black bike's back brake bracket block
broke.

A twister of twists once twisted a twist. and the
twist that he twisted was a three-twisted twist.
now in twisting this twist, if a twist should
untwist, would the twist that untwisted untwist
the twists?

Red lolly, yellow lolly. Red lolly, yellow lolly. Red
lolly, yellow lolly.

Whether the weather be fine
or whether the weather be not.
Whether the weather be cold
or whether the weather be hot.
We'll weather the weather
whether we like it or not.

How many yaks could a yak pack pack if a yak
pack could pack yaks?

If you stick a stock of liquor in your locker
it is slick to stick a lock upon your stock

or some joker who is slicker
is going to trick you of your liquor
if you fail to lock your liquor with a lock.

Don't trouble trouble, until trouble troubles you!
If you trouble trouble, triple trouble troubles you!

Blue glue gun, green glue gun.
Blue glue gun, green glue gun.
Blue glue gun, green glue gun.

Tim, the thin twin tinsmith.
Tim, the thin twin tinsmith.
Tim, the thin twin tinsmith.

Larry Hurley, a burly squirrel hurler, hurled a
furry squirrel through a curly grill.

How much dough would Bob Dole dole
if Bob Dole could dole dough?
Bob Dole would dole as much dough
as Bob Dole could dole,
if Bob Dole could dole dough.

To begin to toboggan,
first buy a toboggan.
But don't buy too big a toboggan.
Too big a toboggan is too big a toboggan to buy to
begin to toboggan.

I would if I could, and if I couldn't, how could I?
You couldn't, unless you could, could you?

Which witch snitched the stitched switch for which the Swiss witch wished?

No need to light a night-light on a light night like tonight.

Terry Teeter, a teeter-totter teacher, taught her daughter Tara to teeter-totter, but Tara Teeter didn't teeter-totter as Terry Teeter taught her to.

The Smothers brothers' father's mother's brothers are the Smothers brothers' mother's father's other brothers.

A bitter biting bittern bit a better biting bittern. And the better biting bittern bit the bitter biting bittern back. Said the bitter biting bittern to the better biting bittern "I'm a bitter biting bittern bitten back"

Certified certificates from certified certificate certifiers.

We need a plan to fan a pan; find a pan to fan, then find a fan to fan the pan, then fan the pan.

How many snacks could a snack stacker stack, if a snack stacker snacked stacked snacks?

Who washed Washington's white woollen underwear when Washington's washer-woman went west?

Mumbling, bumbling. Bumbling, mumbling.
Mumbling, bumbling. Bumbling, mumbling.
Mumbling, bumbling. Bumbling, mumbling

Of all the felt I ever felt I never felt felt that felt
like that felt felt.

Tricky Tristan tracked a trail of tiny turtles.
How many tiny turtles did Tricky Tristan track?
Tricky Tristan tracked twenty two tiny turtles;
that's how many tiny turtles tricky Tristan
tracked.

Iranian Uranium.
Iranian Uranium.
Iranian Uranium.

If practice makes perfect and perfect needs
practice,
I'm perfectly practiced and practically perfect.

How much cash could a Sasquatch stash if a
Sasquatch could stash cash?

Velvet Revolver
Velvet Revolver
Velvet Revolver

How much juice does a fruit juice producer
produce when a fruit juice producer produces
fruit juice? We can deduce a fruit juice produces

as much juice as a fruit juice produce can seduce
from the fruit that produces juice.

How many tow trucks could a tow truck tow if a
tow truck could tow tow trucks.

Slinking, sliding, slithering slyly,
Swiftly slipping through the grasses shyly,
Silent but for swish and hiss
Is the sinuous snake's leglessness.

Peter Rabbit radish robber.
Peter Rabbit radish robber.
Peter Rabbit radish robber.

Sleep sweetly
Sleep sweetly
Sleep sweetly

Purple paper people
purple paper people
purple paper people

Three free fleas flew freely through the flu.

Quick queens quack quick quacks quicker than
quacking quails.

Washing the washing machine while watching the
washing machine washing washing.

Fred fed Ted bread, and Ted fed Fred bread

73

Stupid superstition
Stupid superstition
Stupid superstition

Truly rural
Truly rural
Truly rural

Rolling red wagons
Rolling red wagons
Rolling red wagons

She sees cheese
She sees cheese
She sees cheese

The big fat cat sat on the rat.
The big fat cat sat on the rat
The big fat cat sat on the rat

Ailing Auntie Annie Ames ate apple butter in
abundance.

Double bubble gum bubbles double.

Betty Botter had some butter,
"But," she said, "this butter's bitter.
If I bake this bitter butter,
it would make my batter bitter.
But a bit of better butter--
that would make my batter better."

Billy blows big blue bubbles.
Barber baby bubbles and a bumble bee
Baby boy blue blows bubbles.

A big black bug bit a big black bear,
Made the big black bear bleed blood.

Captain Kangaroo's carefully crunching crunchy
candy corn.

Chris crashes crimson cars quickly.

A cup of proper coffee in a copper coffee cup.

A cheap sheep is cheaper than a cheap ship.

The cheeky Chief Chef Chicken chatted to the
Second Chef Chicken as he cooked.

Chipp couldn't chop chocolate chips 'cause Chip
chipped his chocolate chip chopper.

If one doctor doctors another doctor, does the
doctor who doctors the doctor doctor the doctor
the way the doctor he is doctoring doctors? Or
does he doctor the doctor the way the doctor who
doctors doctors?

Eddie eats eight eggs easily every evening.
Eddie eats eight eggs easily every evening.
Eddie eats eight eggs easily every evening.

A flea and a fly flew up in a flue.
Said the flea, "Let us fly!"
Said the fly, "Let us flee!"
So they flew through a flaw in the flue.

Funny Frank fell fifty feet.

Fresh fried fish,
Fish fresh fried,
Fried fish fresh,
Fish fried fresh.

Greek grapes.
Greek grapes.
Greek grapes.

Grandma gathers great green grapes.
Gray geese graze in the green, green grass.

George and Grace grew glossy grapes and grimy
garlic gladly.

Jackie's jumping jovially 'round Jakarta.

Jumping Jacky jeered a jesting juggler.
Did Jumping Jacky jeer a jesting juggler?
If Jumping Jacky jeered a jesting juggler,
Then where is the jesting juggler that Jumping
Jacky jeered?

Round the rugged rock, the ragged rascal ran.

Raleigh, are you already ready?
Are you really ready, Raleigh?
Raleigh's really ready, Riley.
Riley, Raleigh's already ready.

Rubber baby buggy bumpers,
Rubber baby buggy bumpers,
Rubber baby buggy bumpers.

Lucy and Lacy love lemon lollipops.
Lucy and Lacy love lemon lollipops.
Lucy and Lacy love lemon lollipops.

Rory, the Romanian rural warrior-ruler rip
roared as he rested on his horses' real rear
posterior wrongly.

Rory and Rupert warriors and Roger the worrier
were all really reared wrongly in a rural brewery.

Moose noshing much mush.
Moose noshing much mush.
Moose noshing much mush.

Nine new noisy, nosy, annoying neighbours

Nine nervous Nuns in an Indiana Nunnery.

Nine new neckties and a nightshirt and a nose

Noisy knobbly kneed gnome
Had nine nice nieces

Who knocked nine times,
On a nutty knotty knocker.
The nine nice nieces were known to be naughty,
For eighty one knocks
On a nutty knotty knocker
Is a noisy niecy nutty knotty knocker knock

You know New York.
You need New York.
You know you need unique New York.

Orange jello, lemon jello,
Orange jello, lemon jello,
Orange jello, lemon jello.

Poppa, Poppa picked a pot of peas.

Pirates' private property

Plead Lee's pleas for peas, please.

Quaint queens can't quarrel crazily.

Queenie is quite quiet, but quick-witted.

Seven slippery sea- snakes slithered past the
shore.

Sal sang seven silly songs.

Skillful skaters skidded and slammed against a
big stone slab.

Stodgy students study static structures.
Stodgy students study static structures.
Stodgy students study static structures.

I vigorously sheared the swift smelly silly sheep
on the sweet swell sheep swift ship.

Sixty six sick chicks are stuck in the stock room
full of sixty six sticks.

Sailor Sam saw some swallows swooping
suddenly.

The sailor thought his ship was sinking,
such thoughts no sailor should be thinking.

One smart fellow, he felt smart.
Two smart fellows, they felt smart.
Three smart fellows, they all felt smart.

King Thistle stuck a thousand thistles in the
thistle of his thumb.
A thousand thistles King Thistle stuck in the
thistle of his thumb.
If King Thistle stuck a thousand thistles in the
thistle of his thumb,
How many thistles did King Thistle stick in the
thistle of his thumb?

Vincent the very vivacious vacuuming vampire visited Victor Von Viking the vegetarian veterinarian vacationing in Valentine Valley.

CHAPTER 4 RIDDLES.

What goes up and down stairs without moving?

Answer: Carpet

What can run but never walks, has a mouth but never talks, has a head but never weeps, has a bed but never sleeps?

Answer: A river

What do ghosts eat on Halloween?

Answer: Ghoulash.

Why was six afraid of seven?

Answer: Because seven ate nine.

What's brown and sticky?

Answer: A stick.

What goes up when rain comes down?

Answer: An umbrella

What color socks do bears wear?

Answer: They don't wear socks; they have bear feet.

What type of cheese is made backwards?

Answer: Edam

What happened when a red ship crashed into a blue ship?

Answer: The crew was marooned.

What do ghosts like for dessert?

Answer: I scream.

How do you get straight A's?

Answer: Use a ruler.

I went into the woods and got it, I sat down to seek it, I brought it home with me because I couldn't find it.

Answer: A splinter

What animal keeps the best time?

Answer: A watch dog.

Which case is not a case?

Answer: A staircase

What do you get from a pampered cow?

Answer: Spoiled milk.

Why don't dogs make good dancers?

Answer: Because they have two left feet.

Why was the teacher cross-eyed?

Answer: She couldn't control her pupils.

What to polar bears eat for lunch?

Answer: Ice berg-ers.

Why can't a woman living in the U.S. be buried in Canada?

Answer: Because she's still alive.

That's the worst vegetable to serve on a boat?

Answer: Leeks.

Where do cows go for entertainment?

Answer: To the moo-vies.

What do you find in the middle of nowhere?

Answer: The letter "h".

When is an Irish potato not an Irish potato?

Answer: When it's a French fry.

What do you call a grizzly bear caught in the rain?

Answer: A drizzly bear.

What has hands but cannot clap?

Answer: A clock

Why do you need a license for a dog and not for a cat?

Answer: Cats can't drive.

What room is useless for a ghost?

Answer: A living room.

What would you call the USA if everyone had a pink car?

Answer: A pink carnation.

What would you call the USA if everyone lived in their cars?

Answer: An incarnation.

What did the farmer call the cow that had no milk?

Answer: An udder failure.

What's black and white, black and white, and black and white?

Answer: A panda bear rolling down a hill.

What happened to the lost cattle?

Answer: Nobody's herd.

What do you call doing 2,000 pounds of laundry?

Answer: Washing-ton.

Why do bears have fur coats?

Answer: Because they look silly wearing jackets.

Why can't you shock cows?

Answer: They've herd it all.

If an electric train is travelling south, which way is the smoke going?

Answer: There is no smoke, it's an electric train.

What do you get if you cross a grizzly bear and a harp?

Answer: A bear-faced lyre.

How many months have 28 days?

Answer: All 12 months.

What was T. Rex's favorite number?

Answer: Eight

What can fill a room but takes up no space?

Answer: Light

What's the problem with twin witches?

Answer: You can't tell which witch is which.

What rock group has four guys who don't sing?

Answer: Mount Rushmore.

What's a monster's favorite place to swim?

Answer: Lake Eerie.

What question can you never answer "yes" to?

Answer: Are you asleep?

Mr. Blue lives in the blue house, Mr. Pink lives in the pink house, and Mr. Brown lives in the brown house. Who lives in the white house?

Answer: The President.

Why do dogs run in circles?

Answer: Because it's too hard to run in squares.

What is the capital of Washington?

Answer: W.

What do you call a bear with no teeth?

Answer: A gummy bear.

Why did the Archaeopteryx catch the worm?

Answer: Because it was an early bird.

Why did the cow cross the road?

Answer: To get to the udder side.

How do you make the number one disappear?

Answer: Add the letter G and it's "GONE"

If a man was born in Greece, raised in Spain, came to America, and died in San Francisco, what is he?

Answer: Dead

What do you call a boomerang that doesn't return?

Answer: A stick.

Why do cows wear bells?

Answer: Their horns don't work.

What do prisoners use to call each other?

Answer: Cellphones.

Where was the Declaration of Independence signed?

Answer: At the bottom.

Why does a flamingo stand on one leg?

Answer: Because if he lifted that leg off the ground he would fall down.

What did the inventor of the door-knocker win?

Answer: The no-bell prize.

What nails do carpenters hate to hit?

Answer: Fingernails.

What goes through towns and over hills but never moves?

Answer: A Road

What's the greatest worldwide use of cowhide?

Answer: To hold cows together

What part of the car is the laziest?

Answer: The wheels, because they are always tired.

Two waves had a race. Who won?

Answer: They tide.

What's at the end of everything?

Answer: The letter "g".

I go around the yard but never move. What am I?

Answer: A fence

Why was the strawberry sad?

Answer: Because her mom was in a jam.

What do you get when dinosaurs crash their cars?

Answer: Tyrannosaurus wrecks.

What did the dinosaur say after the car crash?

Answer: I'm-so-saurus.

How do teddy bears keep their den cool in summer?

Answer: They use bear conditioning.

Where does a peacock go when it loses its tail?

Answer: A re-tail store.

Waiter, will my pizza be long?

Answer: No sir, it will be round.

How does the man-in-the-moon cut his hair?

Answer: Eclipse it.

You answer me, although I never ask you questions. What am I?

Answer: A telephone

What is always coming but never arrives?

Answer: Tomorrow

What can you hear but not touch or see?

Answer: Your voice.

Why didn't Cinderella make the basketball team?

Answer: She ran away from the ball.

Why did the baker stop making doughnuts?

Answer: She was bored with the hole business.

What loses its head in the morning but gets it back at night?

Answer: A pillow

What kind of plates do they use in space?

Answer: Flying saucers.

Why did the golfer have an extra pair of pants?

Answer: In case he got a hole in one.

What position does a ghost play in soccer?

Answer: Ghoulie.

Jack rode into town on Friday and rode out 2 days later on Friday. How can that be possible?

Answer: Friday is his horse's name.

What vegetables do librarians like?

Answer: Quiet peas.

What is the last thing you take off before bed?

Answer: Your feet off the floor.

Why did the picture go to jail?

Answer: Because it was framed.

What happened when the lion ate the clown?

Answer: He felt funny.

Did you hear about the origami store?

Answer: It folded.

Why is a tree like a big dog?

Answer: They both have lot of bark.

I have keys but no locks. I have space but no room. You can enter but can't go outside. What am I?

Answer: A Keyboard

If a crocodile makes shoes, what does a banana make?

Answer: Slippers.

What has a thumb and four fingers but is not alive?

Answer: A glove.

If two's company and three's a crowd, what are four and five?

Answer: Nine.

Why was everyone so tired on April 1st?

Answer: They had just finished a March of 31 days.

What did the computer do at lunchtime?

Answer: It had a byte.

Why did the cyclops stop teaching?

Answer: Because he only had one pupil.

What is the shortest month?

Answer: May, because it has only 3 letters.

If April showers bring May flowers, what do May flowers bring?

Answer: Pilgrims.

If the Pilgrims were alive today, what would they be most famous for?

Answer: Their age.

What gets wetter as it dries?

Answer: A towel.

What goes up and doesn't come back down?

Answer: Your age.

What subject in school is easy for a witch?

Answer: Spell-ing.

A woman has seven daughters, and each daughter has a brother. How many children does the woman have all together?

Answer: She has eight children.

What is harder to catch the faster you run?

Answer: Your breath.

What does the zero say to the eight?

Answer: Nice belt.

What type of bow cannot be tied?

Answer: A rain-bow.

What is the hardest part about skydiving?

Answer: The ground.

Why was the math book sad?

Answer: Because it had too many problems.

Where can you always find money?

Answer: In the dictionary.

What has one head, one foot and four legs?

Answer: A Bed

Why did Superman cross the road?

Answer: To get to the supermarket.

What do you call Tyrannosaurus rex when it wears a cowboy hat and boots?

Answer: Tyrannosaurus tex.

How many letters are in The Alphabet?

Answer: There are 11 letters in The Alphabet

What's worse than finding a worm in your apple?

Answer: Finding half a worm in your apple.

Why did the scarecrow win the Nobel Prize?

Answer: Because he was out standing in his field.

David's father had three sons: Snap, Crackle, and ...?

Answer: David

What do witches put on their bagels?

Answer: Scream cheese.

What English word has three consecutive double letters?

Answer: Bookkeeper

What is full of holes but can still hold water?

Answer: A sponge.

What's green and smells like blue paint?

Answer: Green paint.

What is the coldest country in the world?

Answer: Chili.

Why is the mushroom always invited to parties?

Answer: Because he's a fungi.

How do trees get on the Internet?

Answer: They log in.

What day do potatoes hate the most?

Answer: Fry-day.

Where does success come before work?

Answer: In the dictionary.

Do you know how to make a witch itch?

Answer: You take away the w.

What breaks when you say it?

Answer: Silence.

Why did the teacher wear sunglasses?

Answer: Because her students were bright.

What kind of dinosaur can you ride in a rodeo?

Answer: A Bronco-saurus.

A cowboy rides into town on Friday, stays for three days, then leaves on Friday. How did he do it?

Answer: His horse's name was Friday.

What does a dentist call his X-rays?

Answer: Tooth-pics.

What did the nut say when it sneezed?

Answer: Cashew.

I have all the knowledge you have. But I am as small your fist that your hands can hold me. What am I?

Answer: I'm your brain

How does a witch tell time?

Answer: With a witch watch.

What's that gooey stuff in between a shark's teeth?

Answer: Slow swimmers.

Why is a piano so hard to open?

Answer: Because the keys are on the inside.

Take off my skin - I won't cry, but you will. What am I?

Answer: an onion

What only starts to work after it's fired?

Answer: A rocket.

What do you call 150 strawberries bunched together?

Answer: A strawberry jam.

What has one eye but cannot see?

Answer: a needle

What do you call a man at the top of a hill?

Answer: Cliff.

What's a great name for a lawyer?

Answer: Sue.

What do you call a man in a hole?

Answer: Doug.

What do you call a woman standing on a tennis court?

Answer: Annette.

What do you call a man lying on your doorstep?

Answer: Matt.

What do you call a man in the mailbox?

Answer: Bill.

What do you call a woman with one leg?

Answer: Aileen.

Who am I? I am the building with number stories.

Answer: A Library

The more you have of it, the less you see. What is it?

Darkness

Who won the skeleton beauty contest?

Answer: No body.

How do trains hear?

Answer: Through their engine-ears.

Each morning I appear to lie at your feet. All day I will follow no matter how fast you run, yet I nearly perish in the midday sun. What am I.

Answer: A shadow

What has a neck and no head, two arms but no hands?

Answer: A shirt

What is out of bounds?

Answer: A tired kangaroo.

What is the strongest creature in the sea?

Answer: A mussel.

Which type of dinosaur could jump higher than a house?

Answer: Any kind. A house can't jump.

What is put on a table, cut, but never eaten?

Answer: Cards

Why didn't the skeleton cross the road?

Answer: It didn't have the guts.

It cannot be seen, it weighs nothing, but when put into a barrel, it makes it lighter. What is it?

Answer: A hole

Why didn't the dinosaur cross the road?

Answer: There weren't any roads then.

What do you get if you cross a pig with a dinosaur?

Answer: Jurassic Pork.

Where do fish sleep?

Answer: On a seabed.

Lighter than what I am made of, more of me is hidden Than is seen.

Answer: An iceberg

What is the most slippery country in the world?

Answer: Greece

What do you call a dinosaur with one leg?

Answer: Eileen.

A man is pushing his car along the road when he comes to a hotel. He shouts, "I'm bankrupt!" Why?

Answer: He's playing monopoly

What do you call a sleeping bull?

Answer: A bull-dozer.

At night they come without being fetched. By day they are lost without being stolen. What are they?

Answer: The stars.

A box without hinges, lock or key, yet golden treasure lies within. What is it?

Answer: An egg

What makes a loud noise when changing its jacket, becomes larger but weighs less?

Answer: Popcorn

What has a foot but no legs?

Answer: A snail

Where do baby ghosts go during the day?

Answer: Dayscare.

Who earns a living by driving their customers away?

Answer: A taxi driver.

What comes down but never goes up?

Answer: Rain

What building has the most stories?

Answer: The library.

What's a tornado's favorite game?

Answer: Twister.

Why do dinosaurs eat raw meat?

Answer: Because they don't know how to cook.

Why is there a gate around cemeteries?

Answer: Because people are dying to get in.

What did dinosaurs have that no others animals ever had?

Answer: Baby dinosaurs.

What did the duck say after he went shopping?

Answer: Put it on my bill.

How do you stop an elephant from charging?

Answer: Take away her credit card.

Mary's father has 5 daughters – Nana, Nene, Nini, Nono. What is the fifth daughter's name?

Answer: Mary

Why are movie stars always cool?

Answer: Because they have so many fans.

Why did the woman run around her bed?

Answer: She wanted to catch up on her sleep.

What word becomes shorter when you add two letters to it?

Answer: Short

What occurs once in a minute, twice in a moment and never in one thousand years?

Answer: The letter M

If I have it, I don't share it. If I share it, I don't have it. What is it?

Answer: A Secret.

What can you catch but not throw?

Answer: A cold.

A house has 4 walls. All of the walls are facing south, and a bear is circling the house. What color is the bear?

Answer: The house is on the north pole, so the bear is white.

What is as light as a feather, but even the world's strongest man couldn't hold it for more than a minute?

Answer: His breath.

What snakes are good at doing sums?

Answer: Adders.

What do you call a camel with no humps?

Answer: Humphrey.

What's the key to a great Thanksgiving dinner?

Answer: The turkey.

You walk into a room with a match, a kerosene lamp, a candle, and a fireplace. Which do you light first?

A: The match.

We see it once in a year, twice in a week, and never in a day. What is it?

Answer: The letter "E"

What does a sick lemon need?

Answer: Lemon aid.

What goes up but never comes down?

Answer: Your age.

What gets broken without being held?

Answer: A promise

What is even smarter than a talking bird?

Answer: A spelling bee.

What has Eighty-eight keys but can't open a single door?

Answer: A piano

What has a head but never weeps, has a bed but never sleeps, can run but never walks, and has a bank but no money?

Answer: A river.

What's black and white and red all over?

Answer: A newspaper.

What do you call a grumpy cow?

Answer: Moo-dy

What has no fingers, but many rings?

Answer: A tree.

What happens when you throw a white hat into the Black Sea?

Answer: It gets wet.

Why do hummingbirds hum?

Answer: Because they forgot the words.

What did the dog say when he sat on sandpaper?

Answer: Ruff

What kind of hair do oceans have?

Answer: Wavy.

What has a bottom at the top?

Answer: Your legs.

Two fathers and two sons go on a fishing trip. They each catch a fish and bring it home. Why do they only bring 3 home?

Answer: The fishing trip consists of a grandfather, a father and a son.

What do you give a sick bird?

Answer: Tweetment.

The more it dries, the wetter it becomes. What is it?

Answer: A towel.

What do fish and maps have in common?

Answer: They both have scales.

What do you get when you cross a frog and a bunny?

Answer: A ribbit.

Which witch is good when it's dark?

Answer: A lights-witch.

Only two backbones and thousands of ribs.

Answer: A railroad

What did one flea say to the other?

Answer: Should we walk or take a dog?

What gives you the power and strength to walk through walls?

Answer: A door.

What's green and sings?

Answer: Elvis Parsley.

What did one wall say to the other wall?

Answer: I'll meet you at the corner.

What is something you will never see again?

Answer: Yesterday

A man was cleaning the windows of a 25 story building. He slipped and fell off the ladder, but wasn't hurt. How did he do it?

Answer: He fell off the 2nd step.

When is a car like a frog?

Answer: When it's being toad.

Why was the result when a piano fell down a mine shaft?

Answer: A-flat minor.

Four men sat down to play, and played all night till the break of day. They played for cash and not for fun, and had a separate score for everyone. When it came time to square accounts they had all made money. How?

Answer: They were a dance band

Why do birds fly south for the winter?

Answer: Because it's too far to walk.

What do you call a cow that plays a musical instrument?

Answer: A Moo-sician.

What's the biggest problem with snow boots?

Answer: They melt.

Where can you find an ocean with no water?

Answer: On a map.

What has a face and two hands but no arms or legs?

Answer: A clock.

What washes up on very small beaches?

Answer: Microwaves.

What do you get if you cross a centipede and a parrot?

Answer: A walkie-talkie.

What has to be broken before you can use it?

Answer: An egg.

What kind of bird can carry the most weight?

Answer: The crane.

How do fleas travel from place to place?

Answer: By itch-hiking.

What can go up and come down without moving?

Answer: The temperature

What is an insect's favorite sport?

Answer: Cricket

What's noisier than a whooping crane?

Answer: A trumpeting swan

What has a neck but no head?

Answer: A bottle

Which month has 28 days?

Answer: All of them of course

Which side of a parrot has the prettiest feathers?

Answer: The outside.

If you were in a race and passed the person in 2nd place, what place would you be in?

Answer: 2nd place.

Why do male deer need braces?

Answer: Because they have buck teeth.

What's worse than raining cats and dogs?

Answer: Hailing taxis.

Why did the clown go to the doctor?

Answer: Because he was feeling a little funny.

Why did the kid throw the butter out the window?

Answer: To see the butter fly.

What's orange and sounds like a parrot?

Answer: A carrot.

What has a head, a tail, is brown, and has no legs?

Answer: A penny.

Where does Dracula keep his money?

Answer: In a blood bank.

How many books can you put into an empty backpack?

Answer: One. After that it's not empty.

Two silk worms were in a race. Who won?

Answer: It was a tie.

Which fish is the most famous?

Answer: The star fish.

What do you get when you cross a shark and a snowman?

Answer: Frostbite.

What do you get if you cross a dog and an airplane?

Answer: A jet setter.

What is the biggest ant in the world?

Answer: An eleph-ant.

Jack and Jill are lying on the floor inside the house, dead. They died from lack of water. There is shattered glass next to them. How did they die?

Answer: Jack and Jill are goldfish.

What breed of dog does Dracula have?

Answer: A bloodhound.

What geometric figure is like a lost parrot?

Answer: A polygon.

What do you get when you cross an elephant and a fish?

Answer: Swimming trunks.

As I walked along the path I saw something with four fingers and one thumb, but it was not flesh, fish, bone, or fowl.

Answer: A glove

Why don't lobsters share?

Answer: They are shellfish

Does your shirt have holes in it?

Answer: No, then how did you put it on?

What do you get if you cross a canary and a 50-foot long snake?

Answer: A sing-a-long

What do you get when you cross a snake and a pie?

Answer: A pie-thon.

A barrel of water weighs 20 pounds. What must you add to it to make it weigh 12 pounds?

Answer: Holes

A boy was rushed to the hospital emergency room. The ER doctor saw the boy and said, "I cannot operate on this boy. He is my son." But the doctor was not the boy's father. How could that be?

Answer: The doctor was his mother.

What animals are the best pets?

Answer: Cats, because they are purr-fect.

What was stolen from the music store?

Answer: The lute.

I am an odd number. Take away one letter and I become even. What number am I?

Answer: Seven (take away the 's' and it becomes 'even').

What never asks questions but is often answered?

Answer: A doorbell.

When you look for something, why is it always in the last place you look?

Answer: Because when you find it, you stop looking.

Martha Martin was born on December 27th, yet her birthday is always in the summer. How is this possible?

Answer: She lives in the Southern Hemisphere

What kind of coat can only be put on when wet?

Answer: A coat of paint.

What did the cat have for breakfast?

Answer: Mice Crispies.

What do you serve that you can't eat?

Answer: A tennis ball.

I have rivers, but don't have water. I have dense forests, but no trees and animals. I have cities, but no people live in those cities. What am I?

Answer: A map

I have no life, but I can die, what am I?

Answer: A battery

I'm tall when I'm young and I'm short when I'm old. What am I?

Answer: A candle

If a rooster laid a brown egg and a white egg, what kind of chicks would hatch?

Answer: A rooster doesn't lay eggs

He has married many women but has never married. Who is he?

Answer: A priest

What has 4 eyes but can't see?

Answer: Mississippi

What do you get if you cross Bambi with a ghost?

Answer: Bamboo.

What do you fill with empty hands?

Answer: Gloves

Why did the lion spit out the clown?

Answer: Because he tasted funny.

Take away my first letter, and I still sound the same. Take away my last letter, I still sound the same. Even take away my letter in the middle, I will still sound the same. I am a five letter word. What am I?

Answer: Empty

What is at the end of a rainbow?

Answer: The letter W.

What do you call a deer with no eyes?

Answer: No idea

What do you call a deer with no eyes and no legs?

Answer: Still no idea.

What animal is bad to play games with?

Answer: A cheetah.

What starts with the letter "t", is filled with "t" and ends in "t"?

Answer: A teapot.

Which is correct to say, "The yolk of the egg are white?" or "The yolk of the egg is white?"

Answer: Neither, egg yolks are yellow

What is a frog's favorite music?

Answer: Hip hop.

What book was once owned by only the wealthy, but now everyone can have it? You can't buy it in a bookstore or take it from the library.

Answer: The telephone book

What is so delicate that saying its name breaks it?

Answer: Silence.

What do you call a sleeping dinosaur?

Answer: A dino-snore.

Why did the leopard wear a striped shirt?

Answer: So she wouldn't be spotted.

A man was driving his truck. His lights were not on. The moon was not out. Up ahead, a woman was crossing the street. How did he see her?

Answer: It was a bright and sunny day.

They come out at night without being called, and are lost in the day without being stolen. What are they?

Answer: Stars

A monkey, a squirrel, and a bird are racing to the top of a coconut tree. Who will get the banana first, the monkey, the squirrel, or the bird?

Answer: None of them, because you can't get a banana from a coconut tree.

When is it very bad luck to see a black cat?

Answer: When you're a mouse.

What is the easiest way to double your money?

Answer: Put it in front of the mirror.

Is it hard to spot a leopard?

Answer: No, they come that way

Everyone has it and no one can lose it, what is it?

Answer: A shadow.

What belongs to you but other people use it more than you?

Answer: Your name.

The more you take, the more you leave behind. What are they?

Answer: Footprints.

You will throw me away when you want to use me. You will take me in when you don't want to use me. What am I?

Answer: An anchor

What sort of steps do you take if you a tiger is running towards you?

Answer: Big ones.

I will always come, never arrive today. What am I?

Answer: Tomorrow

If you give me water, I will die. What am I?

Answer: A fire

Where do tough chickens come from?

Answer: Hard-boiled eggs.

I don't speak, can't hear or speak anything, but I will always tell the truth. What am I?

Answer: A mirror

Why did the chicken cross the road?

Answer: To get to the other side.

Why did the chewing gum cross the road?

Answer: It was stuck to the chicken's foot.

Why did the turkey cross the road?

Answer: It was the chicken's day off.

Why did the turkey cross the road twice?

Answer: To prove he wasn't chicken.

I run, yet I have no legs. What am I?

Answer: A nose

What kind of room has no windows or doors?

Answer: A mushroom

Take one out and scratch my head, I am now black but once was red.

Answer: A match

I look at you, you look at me, I raise my right, you raise your left. What is this object?

Answer: A mirror

What do you call it when it rains chickens and ducks?

Answer: Fowl weather.

What goes around the world and stays in a corner?

Answer: A stamp

It has no top or bottom but it can hold flesh, bones, and blood all at the same time. What is this object?

Answer: A ring

Which side of a chicken has the most feathers?

Answer: The outside

The more there is, the less you see.

Answer: Darkness

What must we do before we can have our sins forgiven?

Answer: Sin

What has 12 legs, six eyes, three tails, and can't see?

Answer: Three blind mice.

**It has a golden head
It has a golden tail
but it has no body.**

Answer: Gold coin

**What runs smoother than any rhyme,
loves to fall but cannot climb?**

Answer: water

Why can't a rooster ever get rich?

Answer: Because he works for chicken feed.

I am in the center of Paris, at the end of the Eiffel Tower and I start every race. What am I?

Answer: The letter R

What's the most musical part of a chicken?

Answer: The drumstick

I am black when you buy me, red when you use me, and grey when you throw me away. What am I?

Answer: Coal

What is it that, after you take away the whole, some still remains?

Answer: The word wholesome

Why did the chicken go to the séance?

Answer: To get to the other side.

Whoever makes it, tells it not.
Whoever takes it, knows it not.
Whoever knows it, wants it not.

Answer: Counterfeit money

CHAPTER 5: LIMERICKS

Edward Lear (1812 -88) Limericks

There was an Old Man with a beard,

Who said, 'It is just as I feared!

Two Owls and a Hen,

Four Larks and a Wren,

Have all built their nests in my beard!'

There was an Old Man with a nose,

Who said, 'If you choose to suppose,

That my nose is too long,

You are certainly wrong!'

That remarkable Man with a nose.

There was an old person of Fife,

Who was greatly disgusted with life;

They sang him a ballad,

And fed him on salad,

Which cured that old person of Fife.

There was an old person of Putney,
Whose food was roast spiders and chutney,
Which he took with his tea,
Within sight of the sea,
That romantic old person of Putney.

There was an Old Man, on whose nose,
Most birds of the air could repose;
But they all flew away
At the closing of day,
Which relieved that Old Man and his nose.

There was a Young Lady of Clare,
Who was sadly pursued by a bear;
When she found she was tired,
She abruptly expired,
That unfortunate Lady of Clare.

There was an Old Man on a hill,
Who seldom, if ever, stood still;
He ran up and down,
In his Grandmother's gown,
Which adorned that Old Man on a hill.

There was an Old Man of Kilkenny,
Who never had more than a penny;
He spent all that money,
In onions and honey,
That wayward Old Man of Kilkenny.

There was an old man in a tree,
Whose whiskers were lovely to see;
But the birds of the air,
Pluck'd them perfectly bare,
To make themselves nests on that tree.

There was an Old Man on the Border,
Who lived in the utmost disorder;
He danced with the Cat,
And made Tea in his Hat,
Which vexed all the folks on the Border.

There was an Old Man who, when little,
Fell casually into a Kettle;
But, growing too stout,
He could never get out,
So he passed all his life in that Kettle.

There was an Old Man of Cape Horn,
Who wished he had never been born;
So he sat on a chair
Till he died of despair,
That dolorous Man of Cape Horn.

There was an Old Man in a boat,
Who said, 'I'm afloat, I'm afloat!'
When they said, 'No! you ain't!'
He was ready to faint,
That unhappy Old Man in a boat.

There was an old man of Tobago,
Who lived on rice, gruel and sago
Till, much to his bliss,
His physician said this -
To a leg, sir, of mutton you may go.

There was an Old Man of Hong Kong,
Who never did anything wrong.
He lay on his back,
With his head in a sack,
That innocuous Old Man of Hong Kong.

There was an Old Lady of Chertsey,

Who made a remarkable curtsey;

She twirled round and round,

Till she sunk underground,

Which distressed all the people of Chertsey.

There was an Old Man in a tree,

Who was horribly bored by a bee.

When they said, 'Does it buzz?'

He replied, 'Yes, it does!

It's a regular brute of a bee!'

There was an Old Man of Thermopylae,

Who never did anything properly;

But they said, 'If you choose

To boil Eggs in your Shoes,

You shall never remain in Thermopylae.

There was an Old Person of Ewell,

Who chiefly subsisted on gruel;

But to make it more nice

He inserted some mice,

Which refreshed that Old Person of Ewell.

Printed in Great Britain
by Amazon

32791103R00077